What does it mean to have

Attention Deficit Hyperactivity Disorder

Louise Spilsbury

H www.heinemann.co.uk/library
Visit our website to find out more information about Heinemann Library books.

To order:
☎ Phone 44 (0) 1865 888066
📄 Send a fax to 44 (0) 1865 314091
💻 Visit the Heinemann Bookshop at www.heinemann.co.uk/library to browse our catalogue and order online.

First published in Great Britain by Heinemann Library,
Halley Court, Jordan Hill, Oxford OX2 8EJ,
a division of Reed Educational and Professional Publishing Ltd.
Heinemann is a registered trademark of Reed Educational and Professional Publishing Ltd.

OXFORD MELBOURNE AUCKLAND
JOHANNESBURG BLANTYRE GABORONE
IBADAN PORTSMOUTH (NH) USA CHICAGO

Designed by AMR
Illustrated by David Woodroffe
Originated by Dot Gradations
Printed by Wing King Tong in Hong Kong.

ISBN 0 431 13922 9 (hardback)
06 05 04 03 02
10 9 8 7 6 5 4 3 2

ISBN 0 431 13929 6 (paperback)
06 05 04 03 02
10 9 8 7 6 5 4 3 2

British Library Cataloguing in Publication Data
Spilsbury, Louise
What does it mean to have Attention Deficit Hyperactivity Disorder (ADHD)?
1. Attention-deficit hyperactivity disorder
I.Title II.ADHD (attention deficit hyperactivity disorder)
616.8'589

Acknowledgements
The publishers would like to thank the following for permission to reproduce photographs: Corbis/Philip Gould, p.15; Corbis Stock Market, p.25; Zoe Dominic, p.23; Powerstock Zefa/Fotostock, Int, p.18, /Sharpshooters, p.5; Science Photo Library/Gaillard, Jerrican, p.4, /Garry Watson, p.7; Stone/Peter Cade, p.16; Telegraph Colour Library/Genna Naccache, p.19.

The following pictures were taken on commission for Heinemann: Trevor Clifford, pp.8, 9, 10–14, 17, 20–22, 24, 28, 29; John Walmsley, pp.26, 27.

The pictures on the following pages were posed by models who do not have ADHD: 4, 5, 9–27.

Special thanks to: Elspeth, Andrew, Steven, Adam, Yolanda and Joe.

The publishers would also like to thank Dr Marian Perkins, Consultant Child Adolescent Neuropsychiatrist, and Julie Johnson, PHSE Consultant Trainer and Writer, for their help in the preparation of this book.

Cover photograph reproduced with permission of Science Photo Library/ Galliard Jerrican.

Every effort has been made to contact copyright holders of any material reproduced in this book. Any omissions will be rectified in subsequent printings if notice is given to the publishers.

Contents

Any words appearing in the text in bold, **like this**, are explained in the Glossary.

What is attention deficit hyperactivity disorder?

Attention deficit hyperactivity disorder (ADHD) is a **condition** that causes a person to have difficulties learning, behaving and getting on with others. Young people with ADHD have three main difficulties – **inattention, hyperactivity** and **impulsiveness**. These words are tricky.

- Inattention: people who are inattentive find it hard to concentrate on one thing at a time. They have trouble paying attention to anything for very long.
- Hyperactivity: people who are hyperactive cannot sit still. They always seem to be moving around.
- Impulsiveness: people who are impulsive don't think before they say or do things. They say and do things without really thinking about what might happen afterwards or how other people might feel.

Attention deficit disorder

You may have, or you may know someone who has attention deficit disorder (ADD). People who have ADD have some of the same difficulties as people with ADHD. They have trouble learning and concentrating and they may be impulsive. The difference is that they don't have difficulties with hyperactivity.

At school we all have to learn to sit still, pay attention, get on with our work and wait our turn. Until they know they have ADHD and begin to get the help they need, children with ADHD find all of these things very difficult.

Some people find that having ADHD can be a positive thing – you might be able to use some of that boundless energy to help you score the winning goal for your school team!

Getting on with it

All of us do or say things without thinking sometimes, or we find it hard to concentrate or keep still when we should be getting on with our work. The difference for children with ADHD is that things like this happen often and can happen wherever they are – at home, at school or out on a trip.

Facts about ADHD

- Experts believe that around one or two children out of every hundred have ADHD.
- Anyone can have ADHD, but more boys than girls seem to have it.

What causes ADHD?

Lots of people think that ADHD is a new condition. In fact, the reason we hear more about it today is that doctors have become better at recognizing the symptoms and understanding the causes. They think that people have ADHD because of tiny, subtle differences in the way that parts of their **brain** work. In many people with ADHD it seems that the parts of the brain that deal with, say, paying attention, have not developed in the usual way.

How does the brain work?

Your brain controls the rest of your body. It controls how you think, learn and feel. Messages from your brain travel to different parts of your body to tell them what to do in different situations. Inside your brain, different areas deal with different kinds of messages. Some areas respond to signals from your **sense organs** (eyes, ears and so on) so you can see, hear, touch, speak and move. Other parts of the brain are involved in dealing with your thoughts, feelings or memories.

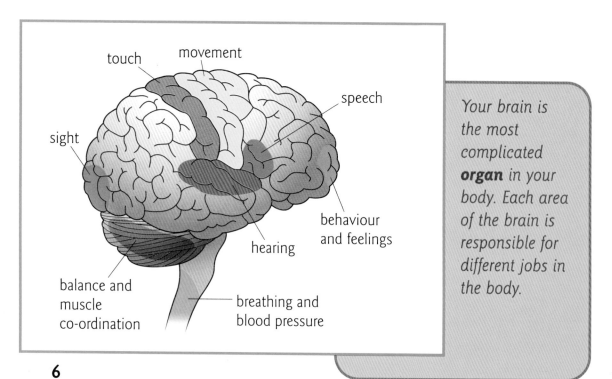

touch
movement
speech
sight
behaviour
and feelings
hearing
balance and
muscle
co-ordination
breathing and
blood pressure

*Your brain is the most complicated **organ** in your body. Each area of the brain is responsible for different jobs in the body.*

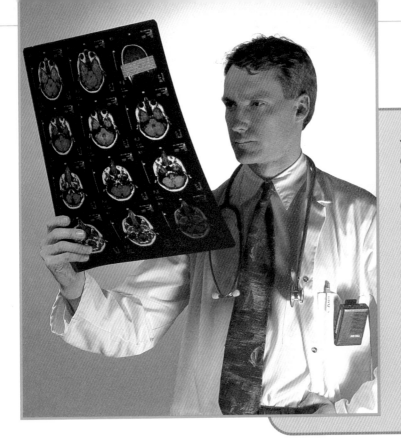

Chemicals and the brain

The brain is made up of billions of tiny **nerve cells**. They connect to each other to sort out information that comes into the brain, work out thoughts and make decisions. For example, when you touch something hot, nerve cells send a message to the brain telling you to take your hand away.

Nerve cells rely on **chemicals** to be able to do their different jobs. The chemicals are made in different parts of the brain in tiny but exact amounts. They affect the way that messages are sent between the nerve cells. There are nerve cells in the parts of the brain that control a person's **impulsiveness**, concentration and awareness of time. Some people who have ADHD have too much or too little of a chemical in these parts. This affects how these parts of the brain control their behaviour. People with ADHD sometimes behave differently from most other people because of tiny chemical differences like these in particular parts of their brain.

Identifying ADHD

Sometimes, parents spot the signs of ADHD when their child is still a toddler, before they go to school. They may wonder why the child cannot sit still long enough to finish a game, or runs around out of control at home and at playgroups or other people's houses. Teachers are often the first to notice that something is wrong. They see lots of children every day and they can tell when someone is behaving or learning differently from other children of the same age.

When a parent is concerned, their first step is usually to take the child to see their local doctor. If the doctor suspects that the child may have ADHD, she or he will send the child to see a **specialist**. These are special doctors who have had a lot of training and experience with difficulties like ADHD. They can tell if a person really has ADHD.

Some mothers of young children who have ADHD describe them as small whirlwinds, dashing around breaking toys and disrupting everything in their paths!

The whole picture

There is no simple way of finding out if someone has ADHD. The first thing a specialist usually does is rule out other possible reasons for the child's behaviour. For example, they may check that the child can see and hear properly. If a child cannot see or hear very well, this may be the reason they are not paying attention at school – not because of ADHD.

When other possible causes have been ruled out, the specialist gathers all the information they can about the child. They talk to the young person to find out how they feel. They also find out how the child behaves at school and at home. The specialist may also talk to the child's family, their family doctor, and to teachers. They gradually build up a picture of the child to help them to decide whether they have ADHD.

Specialists gather information about a person who may have ADHD by talking to them, their family and sometimes their teacher.

What is ADHD like?

What does it really mean to be **inattentive**, **hyperactive** or **impulsive**? Here we look at some of the ways these affect children's lives. All children are different and all children with ADHD have different kinds and levels of difficulties. Some children may only have a few difficulties. People with **severe** symptoms may find it very hard to control their ADHD. Many children grow out of their symptoms, or learn how to control them.

Inattention

Most children with ADHD try very hard to concentrate, but find that their mind moves on to other subjects. For example, some find it hard to do their homework. They may forget to copy down what the homework is, or to bring home the books they need to do it. When they settle down to get on with it, they find that however hard they try, they cannot concentrate. Even though they may be quite capable of doing their work, they fail to finish it, or hand it in full of mistakes.

Some people say having ADHD is a bit like looking at the world through a kaleidoscope. There are lots of different thoughts, pictures and sounds going round in their head, making it impossible to concentrate on one thing only.

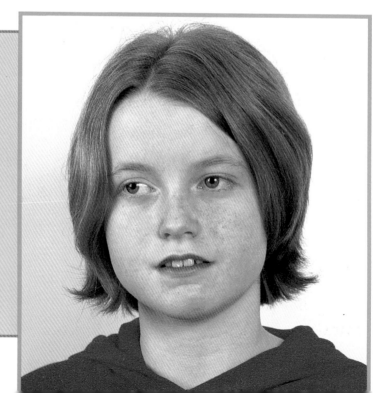

If you have ADHD, you may find it even harder than others to control yourself and you may do things that annoy other people, like pushing in.

Hyperactivity

People who are hyperactive seem to be full of energy. They just cannot sit still. They may dash about, talking non-stop. At school they may be on the move all the time – tapping their feet, getting up and down to go to the cloakroom or to sharpen a pencil. They may try to do several things at once, moving on to a new piece of work or project before they have finished the last one.

Impulsiveness

People who are impulsive may hurt people's feelings because they say things about others without thinking first. They may do dangerous or annoying things because they do not think before they act. They may put themselves in danger, by climbing high trees or running across a busy main road. Sometimes they may annoy other people because they find it hard to wait their turn in the dinner queue or in games lessons. They may push in or hit out when they are upset because they find it hard to control how they feel and act.

11

Meet Lucy and Sam

My name is Lucy and my son Sam is ten years old. He has attention deficit hyperactivity disorder. We didn't find out he had ADHD until he was nine. Up until then he had not had any real difficulties at school. Then suddenly he began to have problems with his schoolwork and he was getting into trouble. His father and I were often called in to see the Head about him.

We thought Sam might have some kind of problem with learning, like **dyslexia**, so we took him to a **specialist** for a check-up. She spent a lot of time with Sam, talking to him and doing tests to see what he knew and understood. She asked his school and us to answer lots of questions about Sam. Sam's dad was away at that time so I saw her alone. I was really upset when she first told me that Sam had ADHD. I was worried that Sam was going to have a really hard time ahead of him. My husband and I took Sam to see a second specialist. She told us that Sam did have ADHD, but that it was not **severe**.

The specialist said Sam should take an ADHD medicine called **Ritalin**. This didn't really help much and he was still getting into trouble. He had some sessions with a **counsellor** to help him understand what ADHD is. This also gave him a chance to talk over how he felt about it all. Sam also saw a special schoolteacher every day for a year, and she helped him find ways of learning that suited him. Then we decided he should move schools. He moved from a small primary school to a large, busy secondary school where children play a lot of sport.

He loved the new school straight away. He seemed to grow out of the ADHD. He no longer needed the medicine or the extra teaching help. He has gone from having real trouble with his writing to doing very well in English. He now plays in the school rugby team and really enjoys it. He still talks all the time – he's a real chatterbox and great fun to be around. He loves music, and comedy programmes on TV. He also loves animals and hopes to work with them when he grows up.

Coping with ADHD

All children with ADHD are different – just as all children are different. Each child needs different kinds and amounts of help. It is a bit like going for a pair of glasses. You don't just get glasses that are meant for anyone who is short-sighted. Eyes are tested and glasses are made to suit the individual.

Emotions can be hard to cope with. Think about how you feel when you are angry or upset about something. It helps all of us to have someone to talk problems over with.

Most children who have ADHD are helped in a variety of ways. Some have help learning to control their behaviour, or advice on how to get on with other people. They may have help with schoolwork, to learn ways of concentrating on their work or completing it. Some children may also take medicine to help them to calm down and concentrate. Sometimes people with ADHD feel that no one understands them. They may feel frustrated that they cannot concentrate. It may help if they can talk to someone about how they feel, and who can help them understand about their **condition**.

Help is at hand

Some children who are told they have ADHD may feel as if they have been given a bad label. They may feel different from their classmates, or feel that there is something wrong with them. Most, however, are relieved to know why they have been feeling upset or frustrated. They are glad to know they can get help to improve things.

The fact that someone has ADHD does not change who they are. Taking medicine and having help from a new teacher are no different from wearing braces on your teeth or glasses for your eyes. The treatment they have is just a tool to help them focus and pay attention. Just as braces make your teeth straight or glasses help you see, the medicine and support given to children with ADHD are just a way of helping them get on with their lives.

If you have ADHD, you may find that it gets better as you find ways to control it. Most people with ADHD learn to deal with the difficulties they have, and to make the most of the things they are good at.

15

Help yourself!

People with attention deficit hyperactivity disorder are often the best people to think of ways of solving their problems. With encouragement, most people can come up with ideas or plans to help themselves.

Many start off with a bit of detective work. They keep a diary of their week, noting down any difficult times they had. Many children with ADHD understand what went wrong after something has happened. The difficult bit for them is stopping it from happening again. With a diary, they can look back to see what caused the problem and think of ways of changing things. They may do this alone or with the help of a parent or teacher. For example, a person may get into trouble at school because they keep leaving their desk. They might decide to try using up some of their energy in other ways. They may do more sport during the day, move around only at set times, or teach themselves to fidget in their seat rather than leaving it.

Exercise is good for all of us, but it can be especially useful if you have ADHD. Doing sport or just running around at break-time can help you settle in class afterwards.

Having a little extra time to do a test can give young people with ADHD a much fairer chance to show what they have learned.

Ways of learning

We all learn in different ways. For example, some people remember things better if they are written down; others are happier to have things explained to them. People with ADHD often find learning hard. They are just as clever as other people – it is just that they learn things in a slightly different way. They may feel happier if they can break a project into several small pieces of work. It is easier to concentrate on shorter pieces and it is encouraging to finish work successfully. Some need longer to finish work than other people. For them, being given longer to complete a test can make the difference between passing and failing.

Lots of children with ADHD also find it helps if they can use a computer. They find that computer programs present information in ways they find interesting, which helps to hold their attention. Some people with ADHD have trouble presenting work neatly. This is not a problem if they can type it up on a computer.

Medicines

Think about how you feel when you are really tired and you have not had enough sleep. Maybe you get a bit fidgety, cannot concentrate properly on schoolwork, feel worn out and perhaps a bit snappy. Then you have a good night's rest, and these feelings go away. For some children with ADHD, this is what it feels like when they take medicine to help their **symptoms**. They find they are able to concentrate and pay attention in class.

Not all children with ADHD take medicine, but some people find that it really helps. There are a number of different medicines for ADHD. Children may take different kinds of medicines in different amounts. The most common one is called **Ritalin**. Children usually take a small number of Ritalin tablets every day. Even if medicines are **prescribed**, they should never be the only form of help offered.

If you have ADHD, your doctor will check on you regularly to see if you still need medicine. Some children grow out of ADHD and stop taking medicine. Other children find that the medicine helps them learn ways of coping with ADHD so that eventually they need less, or even none at all.

Natural remedies

Many people like to take what we call 'natural remedies' – medicines made from plants or other natural sources. Some people find that taking tablets with **vitamins** or **herbs** can help their ADHD. It is often hard to prove whether these natural remedies help, but many people believe they do.

Doing without

Some parents and children do not like the idea of taking medicines for ADHD. They say that children react differently to medicines and that medicines can have **side-effects**, such as making some children lose their appetite or keeping them awake at night. Some children find that medicines don't help anyway, or that they feel worse when they take them. Some doctors say that side-effects can be handled by reducing the amount of the medicine taken. Even so, some people still prefer to work on their ADHD without the help of medicines. It is important that people choose the kind of help that suits them best.

Some children find that taking medicines for ADHD helps them at home and at school. They feel happier and more hopeful because they know they can do some things right.

Meet Jessie and Roz

I'm Jessie. I'm nine years old. When people ask me about ADHD I remember that I used to hate school. When I was seven years old my mum says I wasn't really naughty but I sang and talked all the time and I stopped everyone else from doing their work. I remember that I didn't like the work. I couldn't do the writing and I never finished in time so I had to stay in at break-times to finish it. I didn't care about that because I didn't have many friends then. Some of the other girls in my class said I was silly and bossy and they wouldn't let me play with them.

I don't really understand what ADHD is, but I was glad when the doctor told us that I had it. I was happy that there were other people like me and that the doctor said he could help me. I went to a special small class for a while. The teacher was very nice and never shouted at me. She helped me do my work in bits so I could do it more easily. She let me use the computer a lot as well, and I like using the computer.

My name is Roz and I'm Jessie's big sister. Jessie can be great but she can also be a nuisance. I get fed up with her when she barges in on me when I'm in my bedroom with my friends. Once I got really cross with her. My mum got me to write down all the good things I could think of about her. I wrote down things like 'Jessie is very friendly when she meets someone new' and 'She is very gentle with our cat.' She was really pleased. Now she tries hard to remember to knock on my door. I have put a notice on the door reminding her to knock and ask to come in first.

Jessie and I do a lot together. We both like listening to music and she likes to bounce around in the sitting room dancing. She also likes cooking but it's hard for her to read what the cookbooks say. So I write recipes out for her in simple, clear steps so she can cook cakes and other things pretty much by herself.

Living with ADHD

It can be tough living with ADHD. Some children feel that parents are always getting at them, teachers pick on them and other children don't like them. This can lead to them having very low **self-esteem**. That means they do not like themselves very much. They may feel angry with themselves for behaving as they do. They may cover up or even hide their feelings by pretending not to care. They may become angry and hit out because they are frustrated.

Some people criticize children who have ADHD and their families because they think the child is rough, or badly behaved. The real problem is that they don't understand what ADHD is.

Life can also be difficult for the people who live, play or work with children who have ADHD – their parents, brothers and sisters, teachers or classmates. Brothers and sisters may get fed up because the child with ADHD seems to get all the attention. Classmates may be cross because the child with ADHD spoils their games. It helps to remember that children with ADHD do not choose to act as they do. It's just that sometimes they can control themselves and sometimes they cannot. With the help of others, like parents, friends and teachers, they can learn to control themselves more.

How does it feel?

Although it can get them down at times, some young people with ADHD feel that it gives them special advantages over other people. Many say they are more outgoing and ready for action than lots of other people they know. They are often curious and very determined. The effects of their ADHD may get them into trouble sometimes, but they can also be useful. For example, some people think children with ADHD are bossy because they like taking charge of other people. They may find this annoying, but others may be happy to go along with them. They are glad to know someone who is good at coming up with ideas for games and taking the lead.

Most children with ADHD don't let it stop them doing what they want to do. If they join a drama club, they may not be able to remember enough words to perform in a play, but they may be very good at designing or making costumes or scenery.

At school

We all know how hard it is to get on with our work if something is distracting us. Young people with ADHD find it even harder to concentrate. At school they might not be able to focus on what the teacher is saying if, for example, traffic is going past outside, someone is turning pages of a book nearby, or a clock is ticking loudly.

Tactics that work!

Here are some of the tactics children with ADHD say can help them concentrate at school.

- Sit away from distractions; for example, sit away from windows or doors, or near the teacher.
- Ask teachers to repeat tasks or write them down.
- Keep desks clear of anything but the books you are working on.
- Break tasks down into smaller parts, so you can concentrate on one thing at a time.
- Agree with an adult or friend on a special signal they can use to remind you to get back to work when they see you daydreaming.

Some children find that it helps if their teacher uses a secret signal to remind them to pay attention. This teacher touches the boy's desk as she passes. No one notices, but it reminds him to get on with his work!

Most children with ADHD find their own friends – people who like them for who they are, and who like doing some of the same things as them.

Making friends

Lots of children with ADHD make friends easily, just like other people. Friends can be a big help. They may get annoyed by some of the things a person with ADHD does, but they don't reject them. After all, we all do things that bother our friends sometimes. The best thing to do is explain to people the things they do which you don't like, but say that you still like them as a friend. That way they understand that it is just the behaviour you dislike, not them.

Sometimes children with ADHD get bullied, or even become bullies themselves out of anger or frustration. If you do see someone being picked on or bullied, for whatever reason, you should tell a teacher. If you are worried about getting into trouble with the bullies, tell the teacher when no one else is around. People who are being bullied need a friend and you are doing the right thing if you help someone who is being made unhappy.

At home

If you have ADHD, life can feel a bit chaotic and out of control at times. It can help if life at home has some kind of routine and order. That may mean getting up, having meals or going to bed at the same time every day.

This family has a breakfast-time race to see who can finish first. This helps the youngest child, who has ADHD, eat up in time so that he, his brother and sister are not late for school!

This is not always as simple as it sounds. Some young people with ADHD find it hard to do things at set times. In the morning they may get up slowly and make everyone else late, or disrupt breakfast by getting up and down from the table. It is not fair to them to let them get away with such behaviour just because they have ADHD. Most children just need help to learn to do things differently. Some find that the promise of a treat, such as fifteen minutes of television, is enough to help them concentrate and get on with their meal.

Hassle-free homework

Lots of young people with ADHD find that it helps to do their homework at the same time every day and in the same, quiet place. They may ask their families to help them stop any distractions, perhaps by taking phone calls for them or by turning the television off.

Many also keep a checklist by their table or desk to help them focus on their work. For example, some people who are **impulsive** make mistakes because they leap in and answer questions without thinking them through. Their checklist could remind them to take their time and to jot down any ideas they have for an answer before writing it up. It might also include a reminder for them to ask an adult to rephrase a question if they are finding it hard to understand. You might like to try some of these things yourself!

If you have a book to read for school, it is easier to concentrate if you find somewhere you can be on your own, away from distractions. Make sure you are comfortable as well!

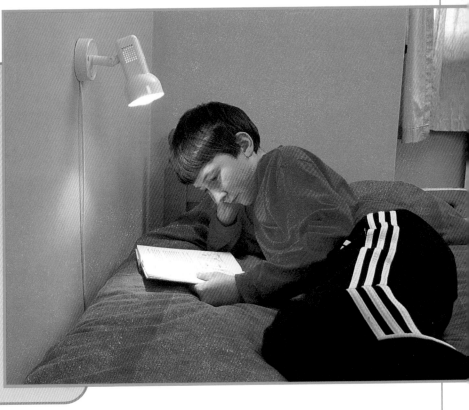

Meet Joe

I'm Joe and I am fourteen years old now. I found out I had ADHD when I was about nine. I was getting into a bit of trouble at school. I went to see a **specialist** who asked me lots of questions and I filled out a kind of form. She told us I had ADHD.

When people ask me about ADHD I tell them that it's not something which is necessarily bad. It's a disorder where you can sometimes be disruptive, and you can lose track of what you should be doing, and you can sometimes be noisy. Sometimes you lose control over what you're doing and you behave in a way other people wouldn't.

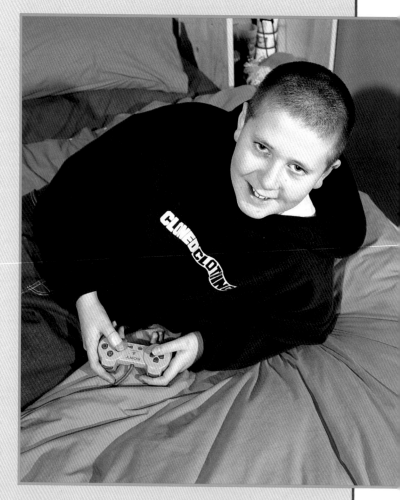

Sometimes I lose concentration at school. I can't always get on with my work and then I joke about. When I get told off I get wound up. My school knows all about my ADHD so if I'm getting stressed out they just say go out and cool down for a bit. They don't see it as a bad thing – they just make allowances for me sometimes.

The only downside about ADHD is remembering to take my **Ritalin** tablets. They are a kind of medicine to help me concentrate and slow down a bit – I have to admit I do tend to rush around from first thing in the morning till last thing at night. I have to take the tablets in the morning, and then at lunchtime, so if I am at school I have to keep some in the medical room. I also have to take tablets at teatime and bedtime, so I have to remember to take them with me if I go to a friend's house to stay.

Otherwise ADHD is a good thing because it makes me more energetic and lively. I've got lots of energy. I don't like things where there isn't much going on. I like being with my friends – I get bored watching TV or being on my own. I like to be doing things. I like most sports, but especially football and ice hockey. One of the things I like most is playing the drums. It's a good way of letting off steam. I'd like to be a drummer in a band when I grow up.

Glossary

brain organ inside your skull. It is the centre of your nervous system and it controls the rest of your body. It tells the rest of your body what to do and deals with thoughts, ideas, feelings and memories.

chemicals great variety of substances which can do many different things. Some chemicals in the brain help to transmit messages from one nerve cell to another.

condition word used to describe an illness or disease that a person has for a long time, perhaps all their life. It is also often used to describe an illness that a person is born with.

counsellor person who is trained to help people with their problems by talking to them and offering advice

dyslexia people who have dyslexia have certain difficulties with reading, writing or spelling. They may also have trouble reading numbers or notes on a sheet of music.

herbs plants that can be used in cooking or in medicines

hyperactivity/hyperactive people who are hyperactive cannot stay still. They always seem to be moving around. Their minds may be overactive as well.

impulsiveness/impulsive people who are impulsive do not think before they say or do things. They say or do things without thinking about what might then happen or how other people might feel about it.

inattention/inattentive people who are inattentive find it hard to keep their mind on one thing. They have trouble paying attention to anything for very long.

nerve cells tiny bundles that pass information between the different parts of the brain

organ part of the body that has an important job. Your organs include your brain, heart, lungs and liver.

prescribe when a doctor tells someone to take a medicine

Ritalin name of one of the kinds of medicine that may be given to people who have ADHD. Such medicines do not cure people but may help to ease the symptoms. Medicines should be used along with other forms of support to help people learn new ways of behaving.

self-esteem when someone feels good about themselves, they have high or good self-esteem

sense organ organ that gives us our sense of touch (skin), sight (eyes), hearing (ears), smell (nose) or taste (mouth and tongue)

severe very serious. Someone who has severe ADHD may find it very hard to cope with life at an ordinary school because they need a lot more help controlling their behaviour.

side-effects unwanted effects of taking a medicine. A medicine usually gives good effects, such as lessening the symptoms of a disease. It may also give unwanted 'side-effects', such as headaches, stomach-aches or sleeplessness.

specialist someone who has a lot of training and experience in a particular subject. Specialists in ADHD know all about ADHD and understand its complicated symptoms.

symptom something that your body feels or experiences that tells someone that you may have a disease or illness. Symptoms of ADHD include inattention, hyperactivity and impulsiveness.

vitamin nutrient that helps to keep our bodies healthy

Helpful books and addresses

BOOKS
Think about Having a Learning Disability, Margaret and Peter Flynn, Belitha Press, 1998

I Am Me And You Are You, Althea Braithwaite, A & C Black, 1999

When It's Hard To Learn, Judith Condon, Franklin Watts, 1998

ORGANIZATIONS AND WEBSITES
Attention Deficit Disorder/Hyperactive Disorder Family Support Group UK
c/o 1A High Street
Dilton Marsh
Westbury
Wiltshire BA13 4Dl
Telephone: 01373 826045

ADDISS (ADD Information Services)
PO Box 340
Edgeware
Middlesex HA8 9HL
Telephone: 020 8906 9068
Fax: 020 8959 0727

LADDER (National Learning and Attention Deficit Disorders Association)
PO Box 700
Wolverhampton
WV3 7YY

The above groups offer support, information and advice to people in the UK with ADHD and ADD.

IN AUSTRALIA
ADDult Association (NSW) Inc
PO Box 472
Sutherland NSW 2232
Telephone: 02 9540 3300

Australian Department of Health and Aged Care
Central Office
GPO Box 9848
Canberra ACT 2601
Telephone: 02 6289 1555
Freecall: 1800 020 103
Fax: 02 6281 6946
e-mail: webmaster@health.gov.au

Index